Margarita Sido

MW00949540

#36 Dove - 51

#12 Fox mask - 21

#39 Butterfly - 55

Easy Origami
for Kids and Teens

#33 Parrot - 47

#47 Crane - 72

50 Models.
First Book Step by Step

#28 Goose - 39

#17 Sailboat - 26

#38 Fish - 54

Origami for Beginners

Origami is the Japanese art of paper folding. Origami is simple, modular and patterned.

In this book you will find step-by-step instructions for mastering the art of simple origami for beginners. All material is divided into basic forms. In each chapter, all the crafts start with one basic shape and are built from a simple craft to a complex one. Don't get ahead of yourself! Working in this order, you will easily master the origami technique, and you will be able to create your own crafts. Origami is widely entering our world. This is an opportunity to decorate gifts with your own hands, create author's postcards and panels, compositions for decorating the interior. As well as, an excellent tool for the development of creativity, imagination, spatial and logical thinking in children.

My long experience of working in an art school with children aged 6-8 tells me that you need to do everything in order. Use paper of different colors on the front and back sides. Arrange the forms as in the photo, follow the instructions. Do not get ahead of yourself and you will master this art without difficulties.

See all of our books, promotions, and new releases at:

amazon.com/author/sidorenko

Messages about typos, errors, inaccuracies and suggestions for improving the quality are gratefully received at:
kostyayaroshenkocat@gmail.com

© 2022 Margarita Sidorenko

CONTENTS

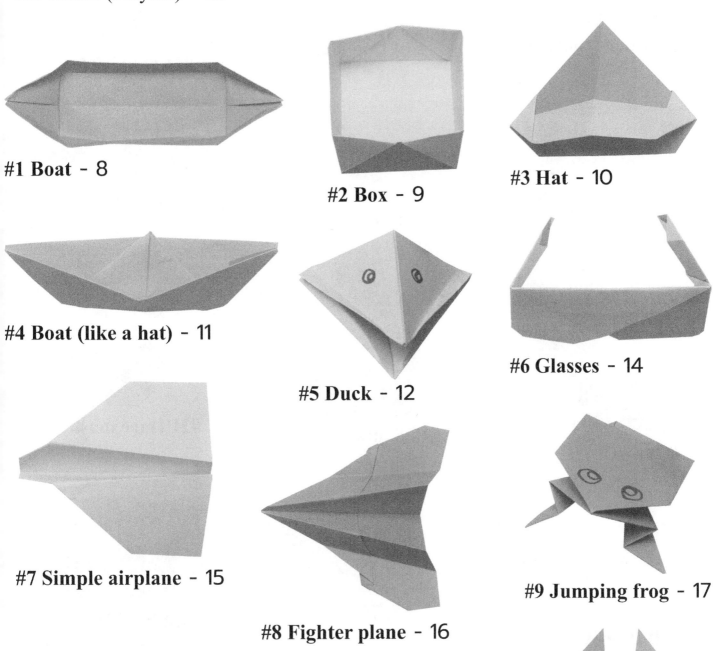

#1 Boat - 8

#2 Box - 9

#3 Hat - 10

#4 Boat (like a hat) - 11

#5 Duck - 12

#6 Glasses - 14

#7 Simple airplane - 15

#8 Fighter plane - 16

#9 Jumping frog - 17

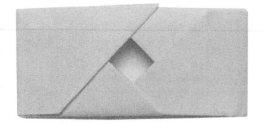

#10 Camera - 18

#11 Lily - 20

#12 Fox mask - 21

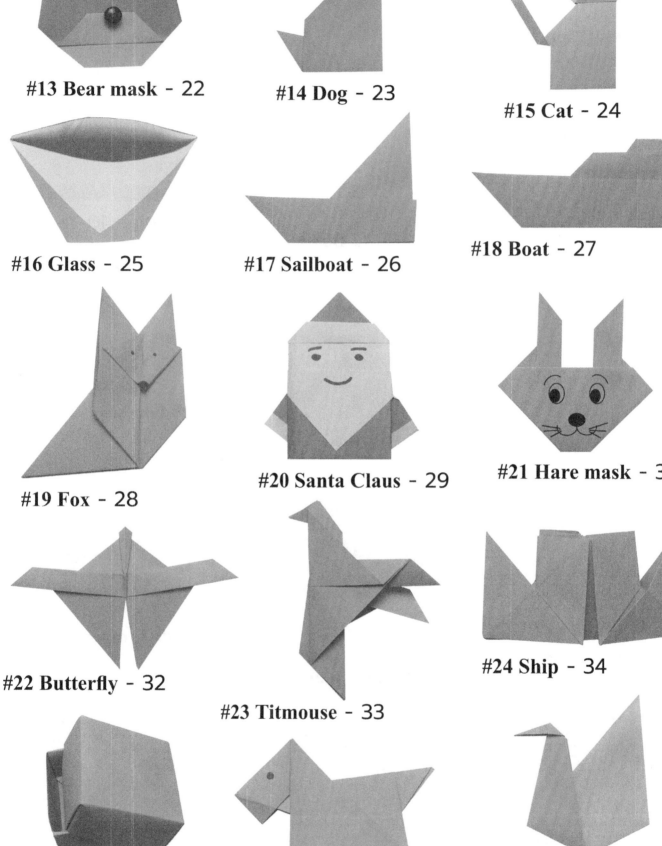

#13 Bear mask - 22

#14 Dog - 23

#15 Cat - 24

#16 Glass - 25

#17 Sailboat - 26

#18 Boat - 27

#19 Fox - 28

#20 Santa Claus - 29

#21 Hare mask - 31

#22 Butterfly - 32

#23 Titmouse - 33

#24 Ship - 34

#25 Boxes - 35

#26 Dog - 36

#27 Peacock - 38

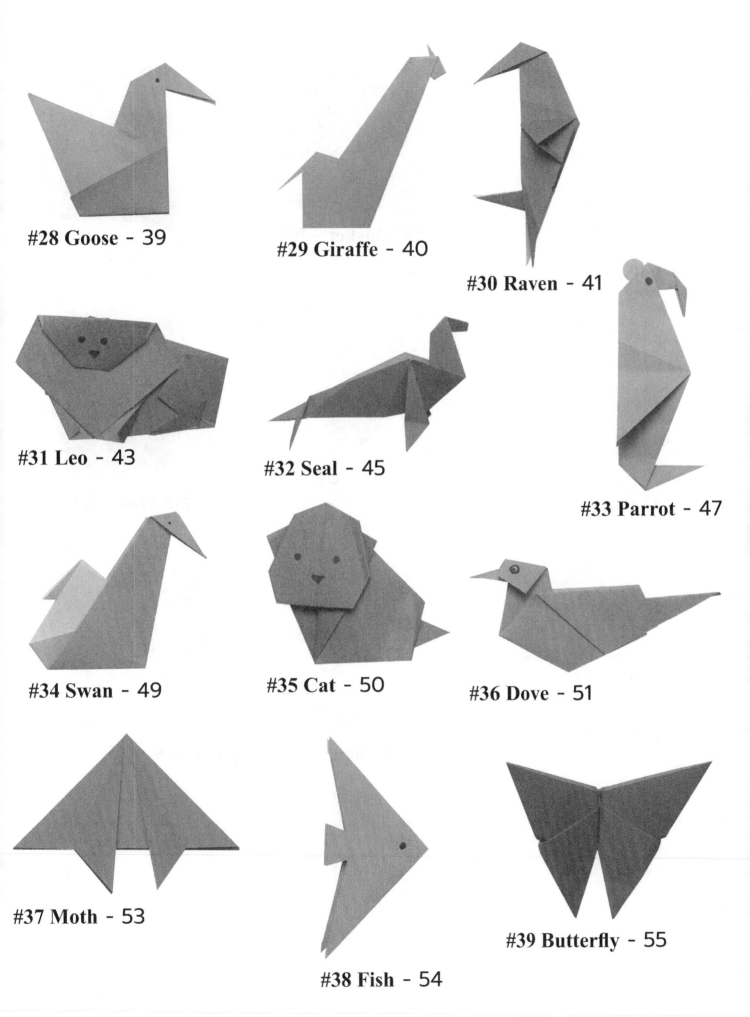

#28 Goose - 39

#29 Giraffe - 40

#30 Raven - 41

#31 Leo - 43

#32 Seal - 45

#33 Parrot - 47

#34 Swan - 49

#35 Cat - 50

#36 Dove - 51

#37 Moth - 53

#38 Fish - 54

#39 Butterfly - 55

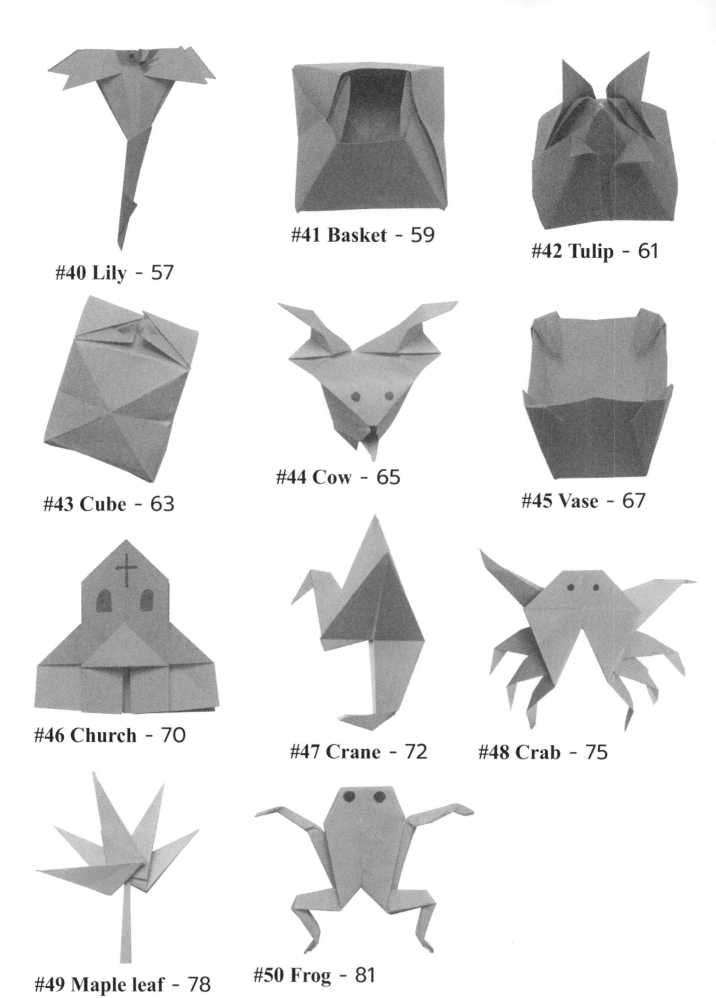

#40 Lily - 57

#41 Basket - 59

#42 Tulip - 61

#43 Cube - 63

#44 Cow - 65

#45 Vase - 67

#46 Church - 70

#47 Crane - 72

#48 Crab - 75

#49 Maple leaf - 78

#50 Frog - 81

SYMBOLS

------- Fold valley (concave bend).

——— Fold mountain (convex bend).

Fold.

Turn over.

Fold and unfold.

Fold in a fold/bend in a fold.

Uncover/open.

Inflate.

Cut.

The **QR code** next to the name of each origami model leads to a video that shows how this origami model is completed.

#1 Boat

Basic shape - Rectangle

1

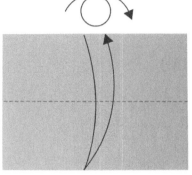

Fold the sheet in half lengthwise. Unfold and turn over.

2

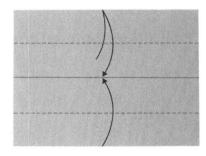

Fold both sides to the fold line, unfold one side.

3

Fold the corners to the middle with an arrow.

4

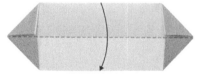

Fold.

5

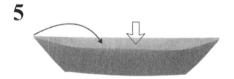

Open and fold the corners inside.

6

Fold the corner of the base of the boat.

7

On the other hand also.

8

Open the boat and fold the edges inside.

9

The boat is ready.

#2 Box

Basic shape - Rectangle

1

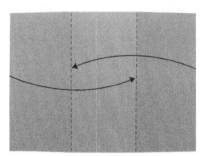

Fold the sheet like a booklet into 3 parts.

2

Fold the top sheet in half lengthwise. Then the other half in half, shaped like a door.

3

Close one half.

4

Fold the corners to the middle with an arrow on both sides.

5

Repeat the same with the other half.

6

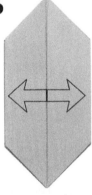

Open the shape.

7

Fold the corners into the box.

8

The box is ready.

#3 Hat

Basic shape - Rectangle

Take a rectangular sheet 50 by 40 cm or a newspaper.

1

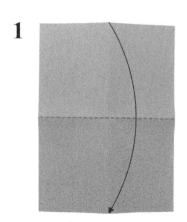

Fold the sheet in half along the short side.

2

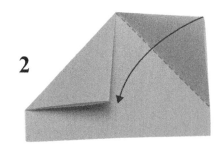

Fold the corners from the side of the fold to the middle.

3

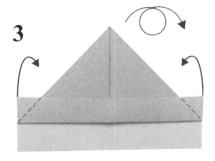

Lift one layer from the bottom up and fold the corners back. Turn over.

4

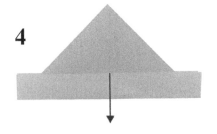

Repeat the same on this side.

5

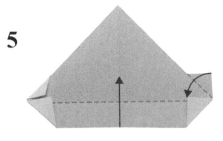

Fold the corners inside.

6

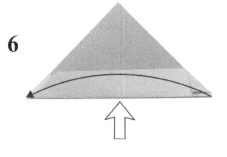

Open the figure and fold the opposite corners, you get a rhombus.

7

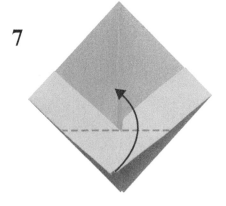

Fold the corners up.

8

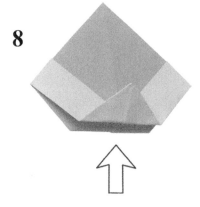

Open the hat.

9

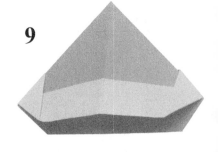

The hat is ready.

#4 Boat (like a hat)
Basic shape - Rectangle

1

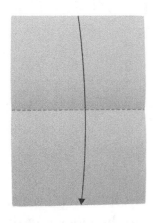

Fold the sheet in half.

2

Fold the corners towards the middle with an arrow.

3

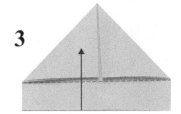

Fold the bottom strip up.

4

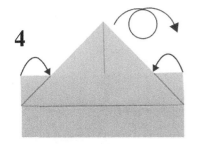

Fold the corners, and turn over.

5

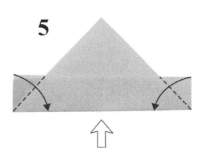

Fold the corners.

6

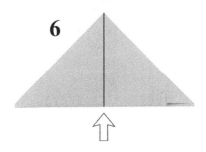

Open the figure.

7

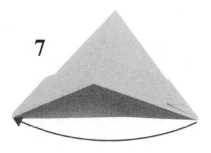

Fold the opposite corners, you get a rhombus.

8

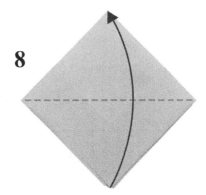

Fold the corner up to the top of the rhombus.

9

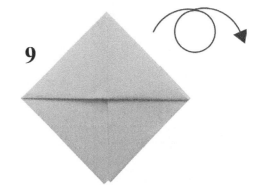

Turn over.

10

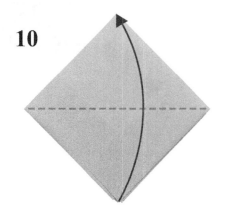

Fold the corner up.

11

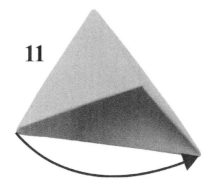

Open the figure. Fold the corners into a rhombus.

12

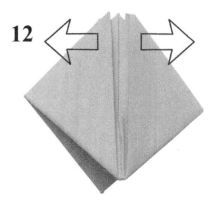

Pull the top corners out to the sides and open the boat.

13

The boat is ready.

#5 Duck
Basic shape - Rectangle

1

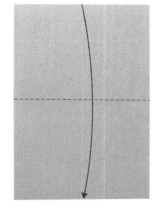

Fold the sheet in half.

2

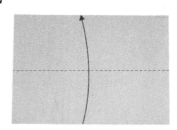

Fold one layer in half.

3

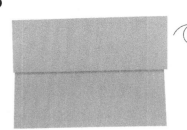

Turn over.

4

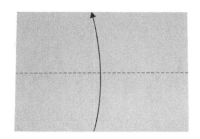

Fold the top corner in a fold.

5

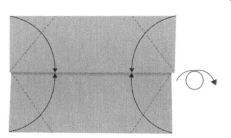

Open one half and fold the corners towards the middle with an arrow, on both sides. Close the half and turn the shape over.

6

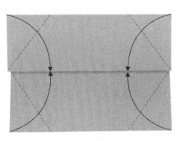

Fold the corners to the center and on this side.

7

Fold the corners so that the figure does not open.

8

Fold the figure in half, corner to corner, and open.

9

Cut 5 mm.

10

Fold the edges of the figure relative to the cut.

11

Open the figure and fold the corners. You can draw eyes, stick a tongue, decorate to your liking.

#6 Glasses
Basic shape - Rectangle

1

Fold the sheet along the line that connects the opposite corners of the sheet.

2

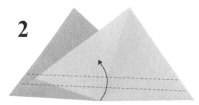

Fold the edge with the fold line up two times.

3

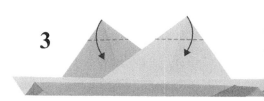

Fold the corners.

4

Fold the strips towards the middle.

5

6

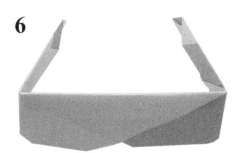

Glasses are ready.

#7 Simple airplane
Basic shape - Rectangle

With such an airplane, you can send messages to each other by airmail.

1

2

Fold the top two corners towards the middle with an arrow.

3

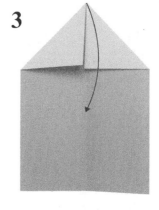

Fold the corner down.

4

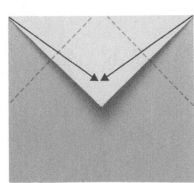

Fold the corners to the middle again, leaving a small distance from above, and from below the corners close.

5

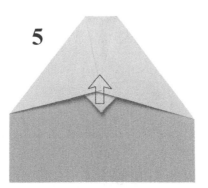

Fold the resulting corner in the center of the figure up.

6

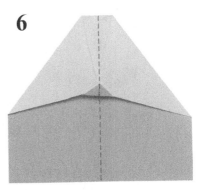

Fold.

7

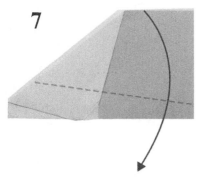

Fold the edges up like wings on both sides.

8

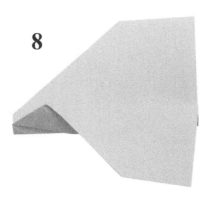

9

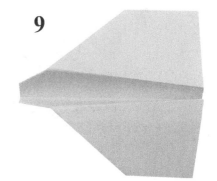

And flew...

#8 Fighter plane
Basic shape - Rectangle

1

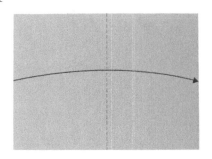

Fold the sheet in half along the short side.

2

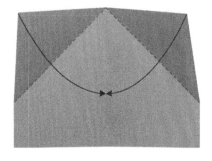

Fold up. Fold the corners towards the middle.

3

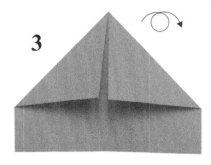

Turn over to the other side.

4

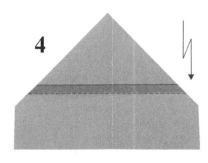

Fold the top corner down and back to form a crease.

5

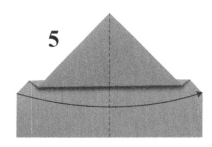

Fold in half.

6

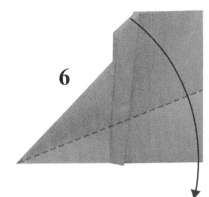

Fold the halves from an acute angle like wings.

7

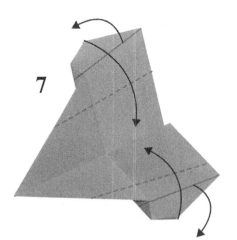

Fold each wing into a crease.

8

9

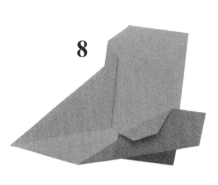

The plane is ready.

#9 Jumping frog
Basic shape - Rectangle

The frog jumps if you push your finger on the fold and release it sharply.

1

Fold the corner.

2

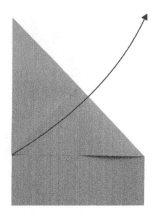

Unfold.

3

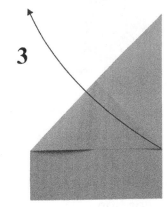

Fold the other, unfold, turn over.

4

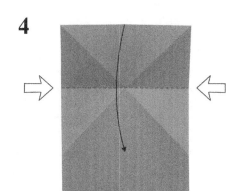

Fold and unfold.

5

Complete along the fold lines.

6

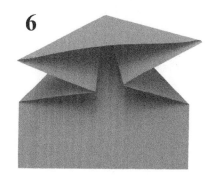

7

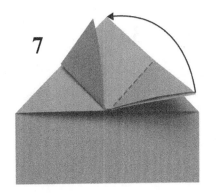

Fold the corners up.

8

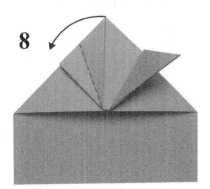

Fold the corners.

9

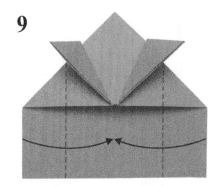

Fold the sides to the middle of the figure.

17

10

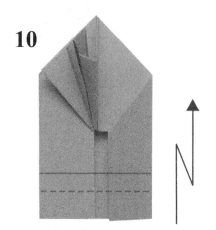

Fold the bottom with an accordion.

11

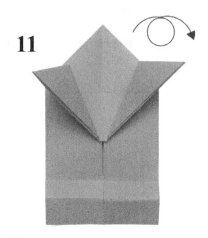

Turn over.

12

Done.

#10 Camera
Basic shape - Rectangle

1

Take a sheet of 20cm by 30cm.

2

Cut into 4 pieces.

3

Fold each piece in half lengthwise and unfold.

4

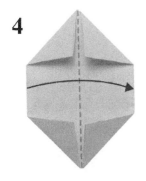

Fold the corners with an arrow and fold.

5

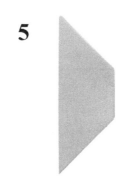

Make 4 workpieces.

6

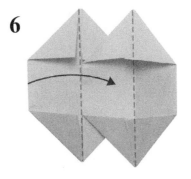

Fold two blanks and close one half.

7

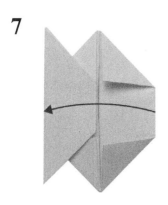

Then another.

8

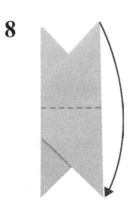

Fold the workpiece in half across.

9

Fold another piece like this.

10

Insert the sharp corners of the parts one inside the other inside.

11

The right and left parts of the camera should move apart easily, forming a hole lens.

12

The camera is ready.

#11 Lily
Basic shape - Triangle

1

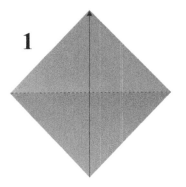

2

Fold the triangle in half, connecting sharp corners and unfold.

3

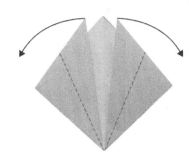

Fold the corners up to the top. Fold both triangles in half.

4

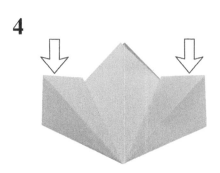

Open these triangles from the inside and flatten along the fold lines, pressing in the middle.

5

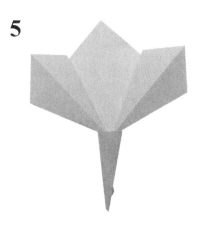

It turned out a lily, add a stalk by rolling a strip of green paper into a tube.

20

#12 Fox mask
Basic shape - Triangle

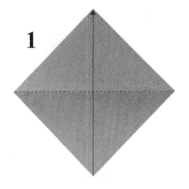

1

2

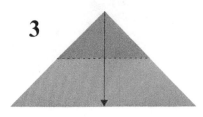

3

Fold the top corner down.

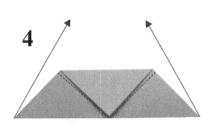

4

Fold the sharp corners up - ears.

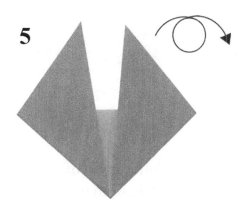

5

Turn the shape over.

6

Draw the eyes and nose.

#13 Bear mask

Basic shape - Triangle

1

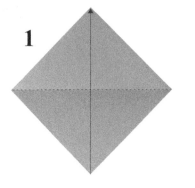

2

Fold the corner.

3

Fold the corner in the opposite direction so that you get a crease.

4

5

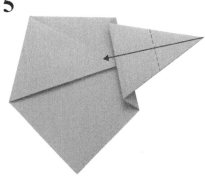

Fold the tip of the corner - this is an ear.

6

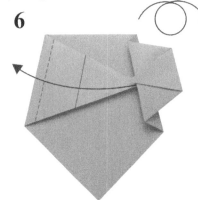

Make a second ear and turn over.

7

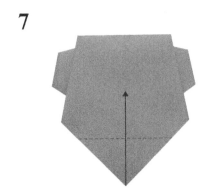

Fold the corner up.

8

Fold down one layer.

9

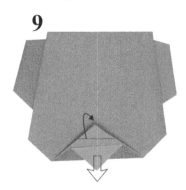

Fold the corner inside.

10

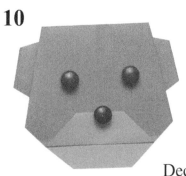

Decorate the face.

#14 Dog
Basic shape - Triangle

Square sheet 7x7 or 12x12
- 2 pieces.

1

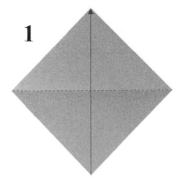

2

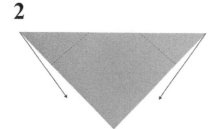

Fold the sharp corners
of the triangle down
towards the right angle.

3

Fold the corners in half
lengthwise.

4

Open the corners from
the inside and flatten the
corners.

5

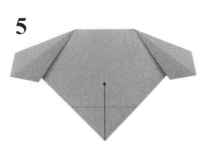

Fold up the corner.

6

Draw the eyes and nose.

7

Take the second triangle
and fold the corner parallel
to the bottom side.

8

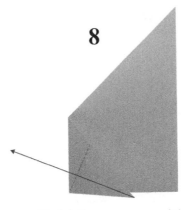

Fold the corner with a
crease.

9

Open the square
completely.

10

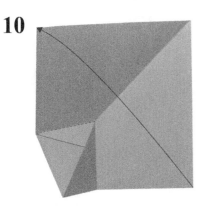

Fold the valley fold into
the mountain fold.

11

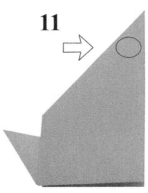

Open the triangle along
the fold lines, spread
with glue.

12

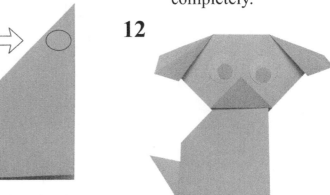

Glue the head to the
body.

23

#15 Cat

Basic shape - Triangle

1

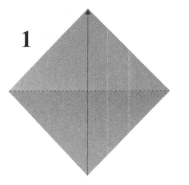

2

Fold the sharp corners of
the triangle.

3

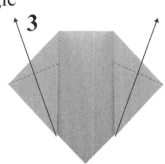

Fold the corners up with
a crease, ears.

4

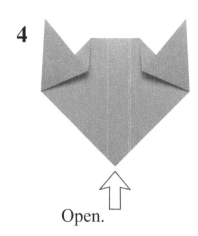

Open.

5

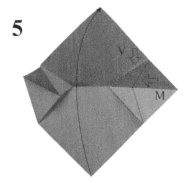
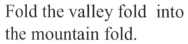

Fold the valley fold into
the mountain fold.

6

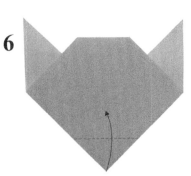

Fold the ears inside, fold
the corner up.

7

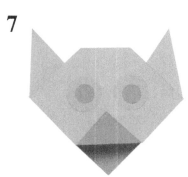

Draw the eyes and nose.

8

Take the second triangle.
Fold the bottom corner
parallel to the bottom side.

9

Cut the strip parallel to
the fold line.

10

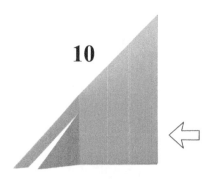

Open the triangle.

11

Fold the corners in and
complete.

12

Glue the head and the cat
is ready.

#16 Glass
Basic shape - Triangle

1

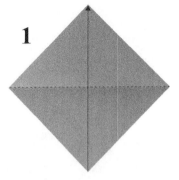

Fold the corner to the opposite side of the triangle.

2

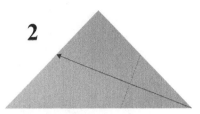

Raise the corner to the opposite side of the triangle.

3

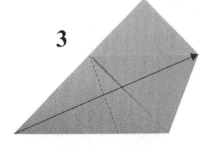

Also fold the second corner

4

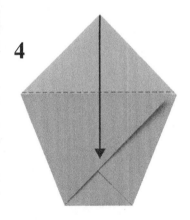

One layer of corner fold down.

5

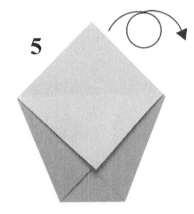

Turn the figure over.

6

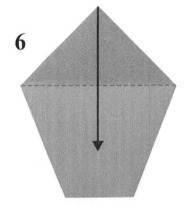

Fold the second sheet of a right angle down.

7

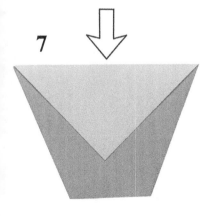

Open the figure.

8

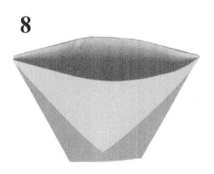

The glass is ready.

#17 Sailboat
Basic shape - Triangle

1

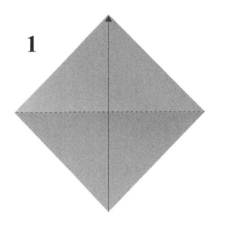

2

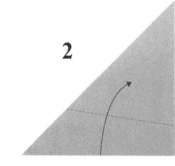

Fold the bottom side up.

3

Open the square
completely.

4

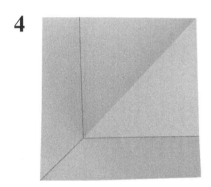

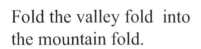

Fold the valley fold into
the mountain fold.

5

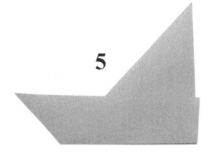

Complete the figure
along the fold lines.

#18 Boat
Basic shape - Triangle

1

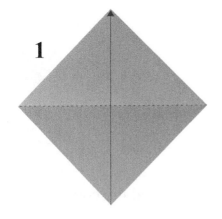

2

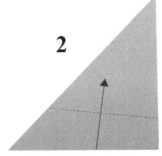

Fold the bottom side up.

3

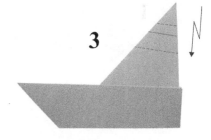

Fold the upper sharp corner down and then up with a fold and down again.

4

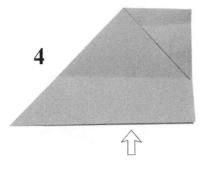

Open the square completely.

5

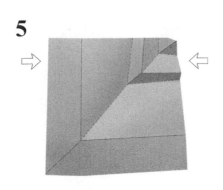

Fold the valley fold into the mountain fold.

6

Complete the figure along the fold lines.

#19 Fox
Basic shape - Triangle

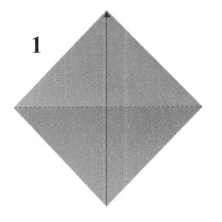
1

2

Fold the corner up to the top of the triangle.

3

Fold the corner.

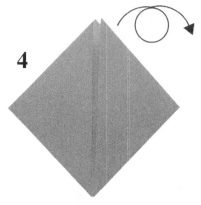
4

Turn over.

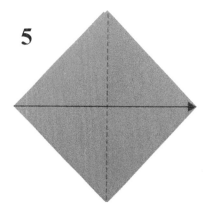
5

Fold in half vertically.

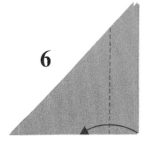
6

Open the triangle with the fold down and fold half of the triangle.

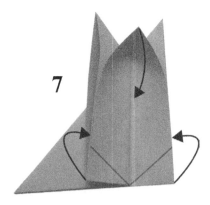
7

Fold the bottom corners back.

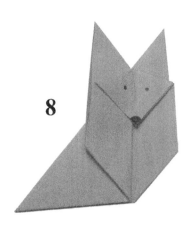
8

Fold the middle part down and shape the face of the fox.

#20 Santa Claus
Basic shape - Triangle

1

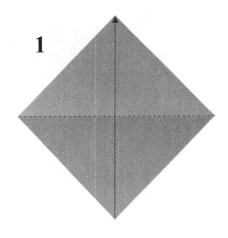

2

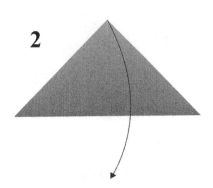

Fold the triangle.

3

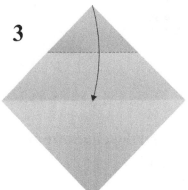

Fold the corner down to the fold line.

4

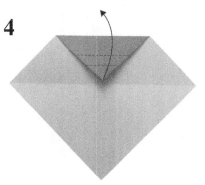

Fold up the corner.

5

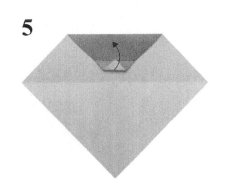

Fold up again.

6

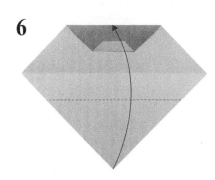

Fold the bottom corner.

7

Fold down.

8

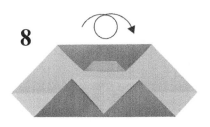

Turn over.

9

Fold the strips from the edge.

29

10

Fold the edges from the top.

11

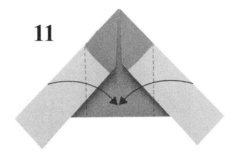

Fold vertically.

12

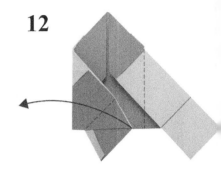

Fold up to the side - sleev

13

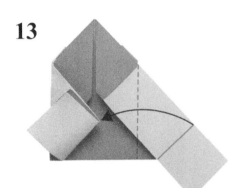

Fold, on the other hand, vertically.

14

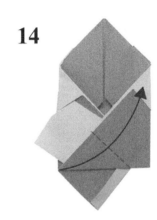

Fold to the side.

15

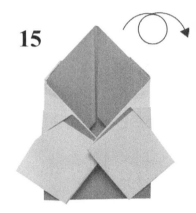

Turn over.

16

Merry Christmas!

#21 Hare mask
Basic shape - Fold

1

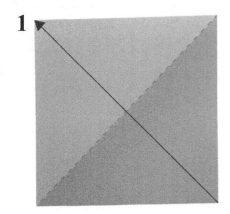

Fold.

2

Fold the fold line by 1-2 cm.

3

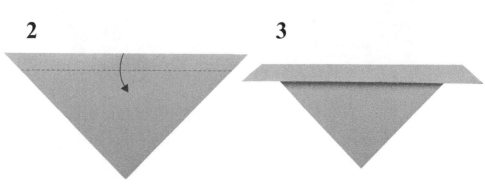

4

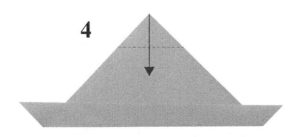

Fold the top corner down
to the crease.

5

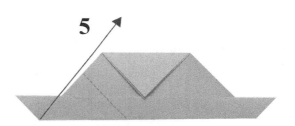

Fold the corner up.

6

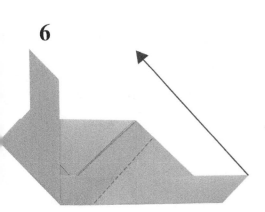

Fold the corner up, leave
the distance between
them- the ears.

7

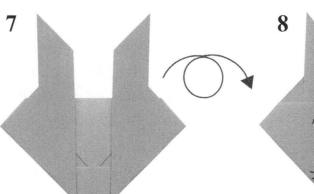

Turn the mask over.

8

Draw a face.

#22 Butterfly
Basic shape - Fold

1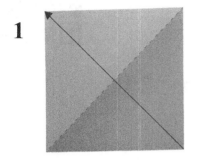

Fold.

2

Fold the fold line by 1-2 cm.

3

4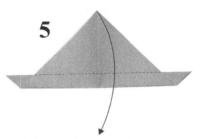

Fold the form in half and unfold.

5

Fold one layer of the corner down.

6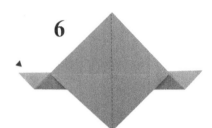

Fold in half.

7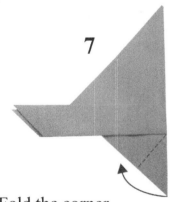

Fold the corner.

8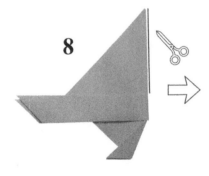

Cut along the fold line to the crease. Open the shape.

9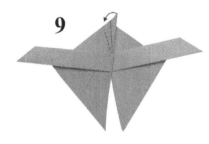

Fold the corner in half again and flatten.

10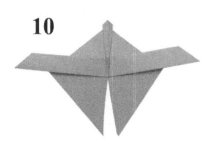

#23 Titmouse
Basic shape - Fold

1

Fold.

2

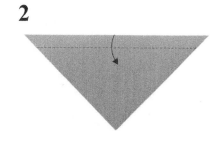

Fold the fold line by 1-2 cm.

3

4

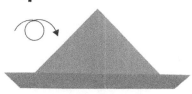

Turn over.

5

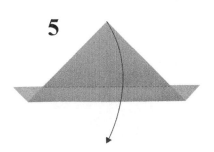

Fold the triangle down.

6

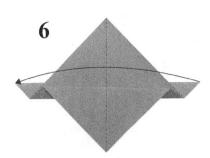

Fold in half.

7

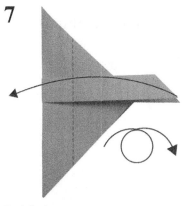

Fold the crease at an angle and turn it over.

8

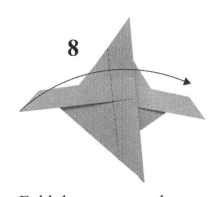

Fold the crease so that the wings do not match.

9

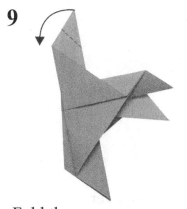

Fold the corner.

10

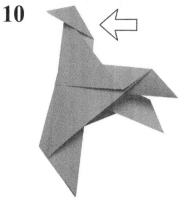

Open and wrap the beak on both sides.

11

#24 Ship

Basic shape - Envelope

1

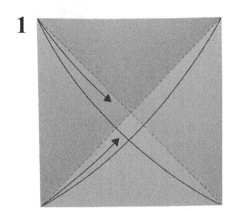

Fold the square into an angle, unfold. Fold to another corner and unfold.

2

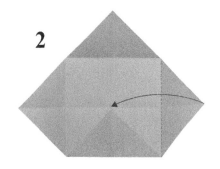

Fold the corners.

3

Turn over.

4

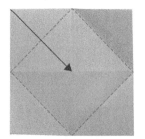

Fold the corners to the center.

5

Turn over.

6

Fold up the third time.

7

Turn over.

8

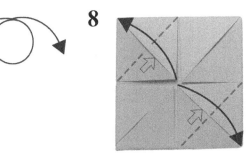

Open two pockets.

9

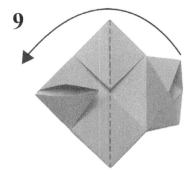

Fold in half.

10

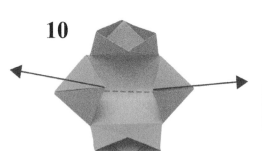

Fold the corners.

11

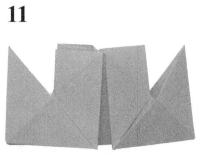

The ship is ready.

34

#25 Boxes
Basic shape - Envelope

1

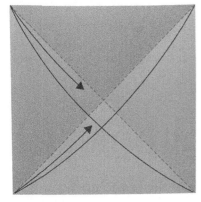

Fold the square into an angle, unfold. Fold to another corner and unfold.

2

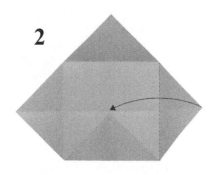

Fold the corners to the center.

3

4

Fold 2 envelopes. One is slightly larger than the other.

5

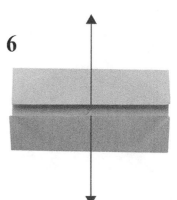

Fold the edge into the middle.

6

Fold the other edge into the middle.

7

Unfold and fold the edges vertically.

8

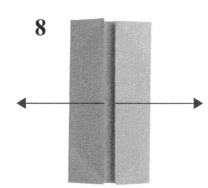

Unfold.

9

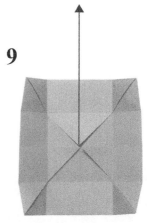

Open one corner.

10

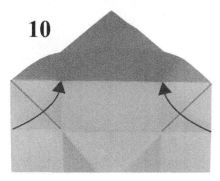

Fold the corners inwards, lifting the side edges.

11

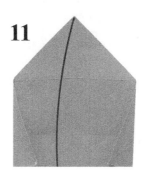

Turn the corner inside.

12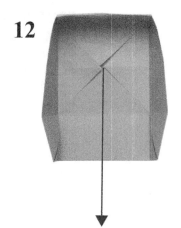

Unfold the opposite corner.

13

Fold the corners inwards, lifting the side edges.

14

Fold the corner inside.

15

Fold the second envelope as well.

16

It turned out two boxes, the bottom and the lid.

17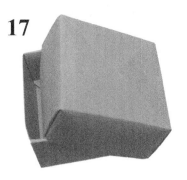

The box is ready.

#26 Dog
Basic shape - Envelope

1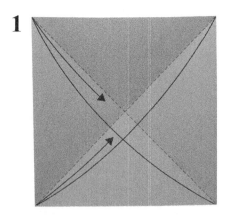

Fold the square into an angle, unfold. Fold to another corner and unfold.

2

Fold the corners to the center.

3

4

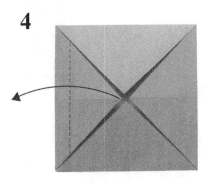

Fold the corner of the folding.

5

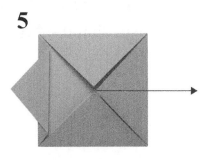

Fold the corner.

6

Fold it to the fold line and close it back.

7

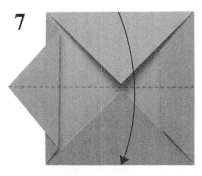

Fold in half.

8

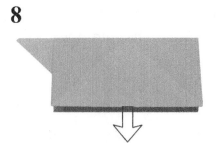

Straighten the corners down.

9

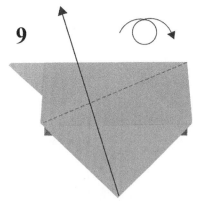

Fold up and turn over.

10

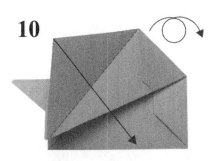

Fold the corner down and turn over, close the corner.

11

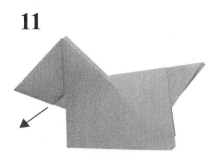

Straighten the angle from the bottom to the outside.

12

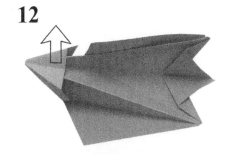

Unfold the shape from the bottom and open.

13

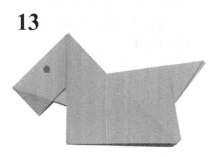

The dog is ready.

#27 Peacock
Basic shape - Arrow

1

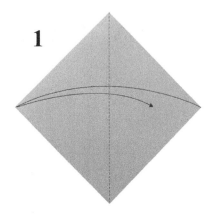

2

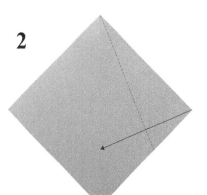

Fold the sides of the
square to the fold line.

3

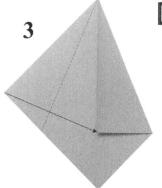

4

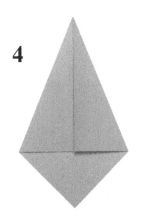

5

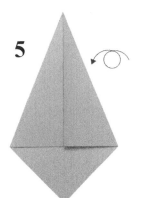

Turn over.

6

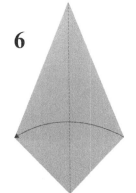

Fold in half.

7

Fold the corner twice.

8

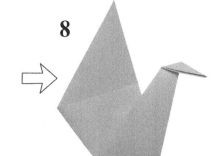

Open the shape.

9

Fold the mountain fold
into the valley fold.
Complete the shape by
the folds.

10

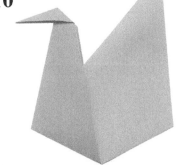

#28 Goose
Basic shape - Arrow

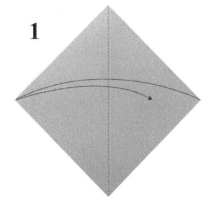

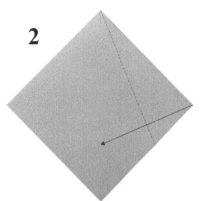

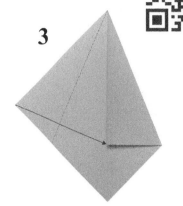

Fold the sides of the
square to the fold line.

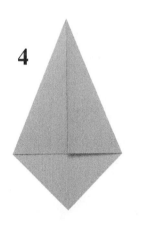

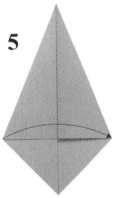

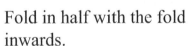

Fold the corner 2 times.

Fold in half with the fold
inwards.

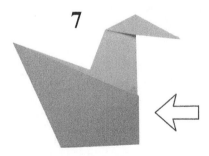

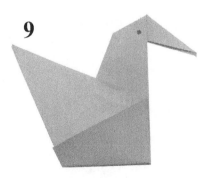

Open the shape.

The goose turned out.

Change the folds mountain
and valley.
Complete along the fold lines.

#29 Giraffe
Basic shape - Arrow

1

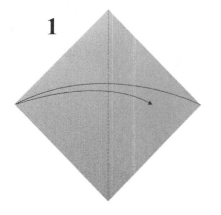

2

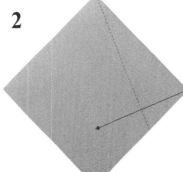

3

Fold the sides of the square to the fold line.

4

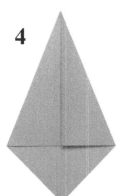

5

Fold in half with the fold inwards.

6

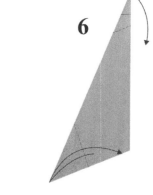

Fold the sharp corner of the folding, fold the bottom corner.

7

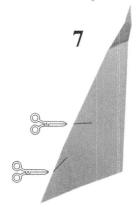

Incision.

8

Fold the incisions.

9

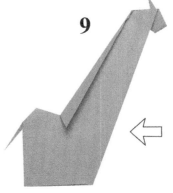

Open the shape.

10

Fold the bends into valleys.

11

Complete the shape.

#30 Raven
Basic shape - Arrow

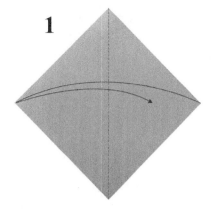

1

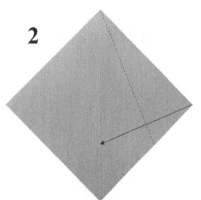

2

Fold the sides of the
square to the fold line.

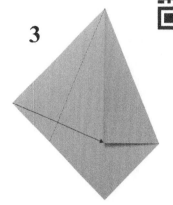

3

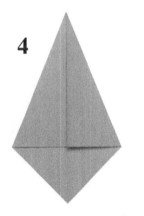

4

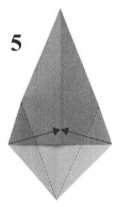

5

Fold the lower sides to
the center.

6

Open the square.

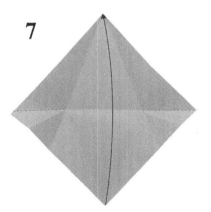

7

Fold the triangle across
to fold the corners.

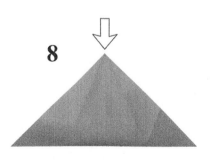

8

Open.

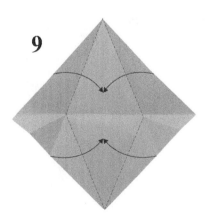

9

Fold the arrows at the
same time leaving the
triangles in the middle.

10

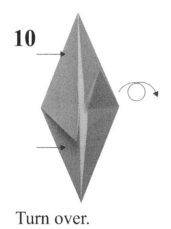

Turn over.

11

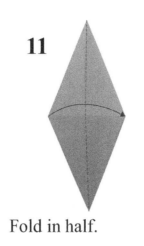

Fold in half.

12

Incision.

13

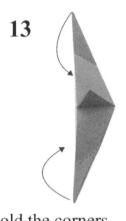

Fold the corners.

14

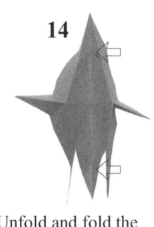
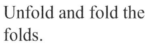

Unfold and fold the folds.

15

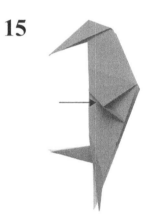

Complete the form, fold the wings and paws.

16

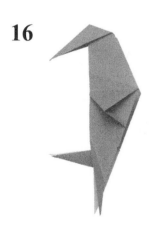

#31 Leo
Basic shape - Arrow

1

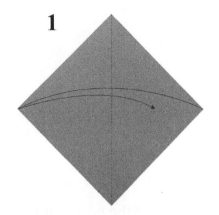

2

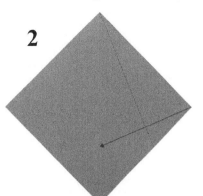

Fold the sides of the
square to the fold line.

3

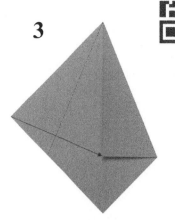

4

5

Fold the corners.

6

Fold in half.

7

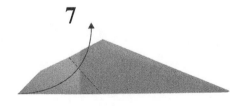

Fold the corner up.

8

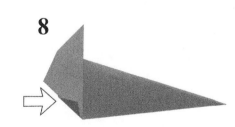

Open.

9

Fold the folds.

10

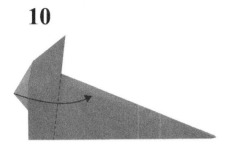

Complete the shape and fold one half to the side.

11

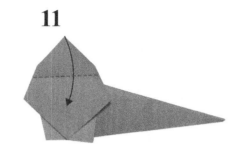

Fold the upper corner.

12

Fold the corner inwards and make a crease at the end of the acute angle.

13

Fold the corners – paws and tail.

14

Draw a face.

#32 Seal
Basic shape - Arrow

1

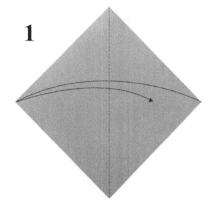

2

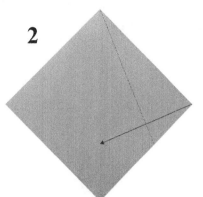

Fold the sides of the square to the fold line.

3

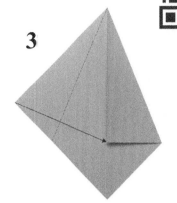

4

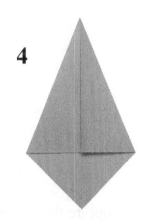

5

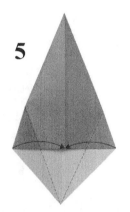

Fold the lower sides to the center.

6

Open.

7

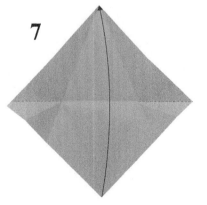

Fold across.

8

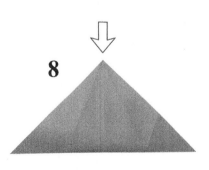

Open.

9

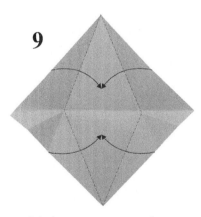

Fold the arrows at the same time leaving the triangles in the middle.

10

Turn over.

11

Fold in half.

12

Fold the corners, cut.

13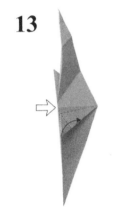

Fold and unfold.

14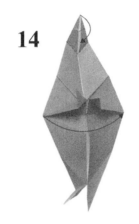

Fold the bends into
valleys and mountains.

15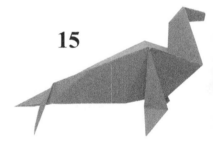

Complete the shape. fold
the fins in half and up.

46

#33 Parrot

Basic shape - Arrow

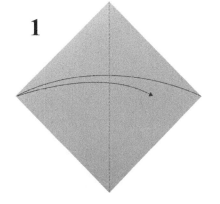

1

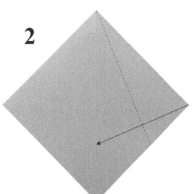

2

Fold the sides of the square to the fold line.

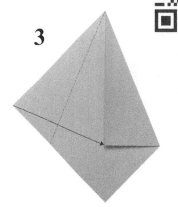

3

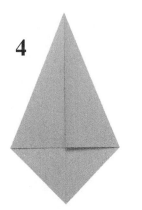

4

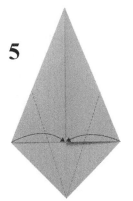

5

Fold the lower sides to the center.

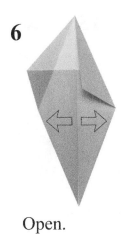

6

Open.

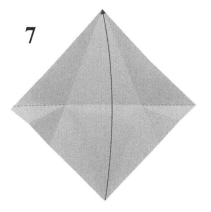

7

Fold across.

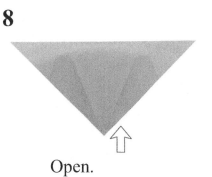

8

Open.

9

Fold the arrows at the same time leaving the triangles in the middle.

10

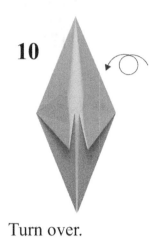

Turn over.

11

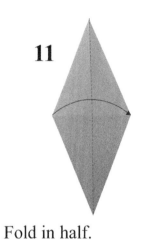

Fold in half.

12

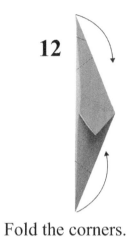

Fold the corners.

13

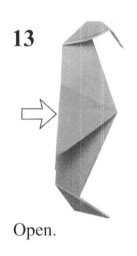

Open.

14

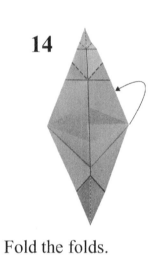

Fold the folds.

15

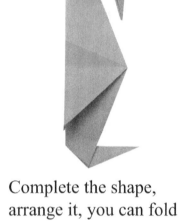

Complete the shape,
arrange it, you can fold
the wings and paws.

#34 Swan
Basic shape - Arrow

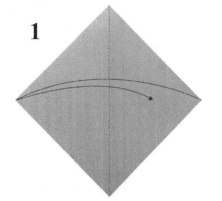

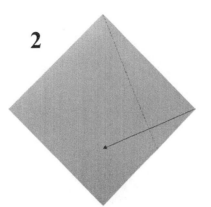

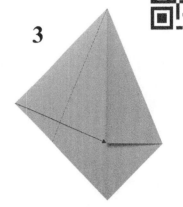

Fold the sides of the square to the fold line.

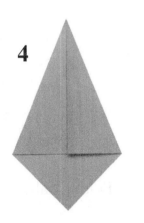

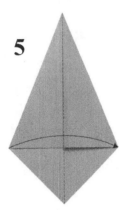

Fold in half.

Fold the corners.

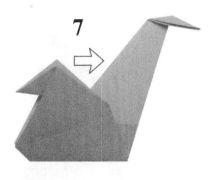

Open.

Fold the bends into valleys and mountains.

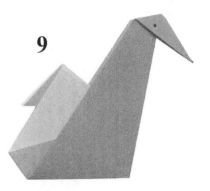

Complete the figure.

49

#35 Cat

Basic shape - Arrow

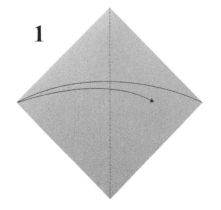

1

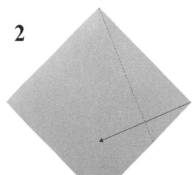

2

Fold the sides of the
square to the fold line.

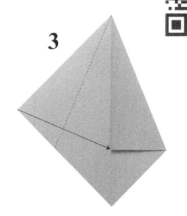

3

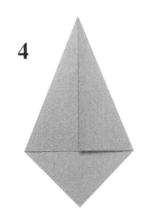

4

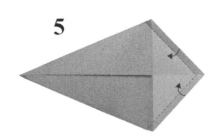

5

Fold the edges.

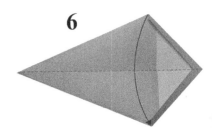

6

Fold in half.

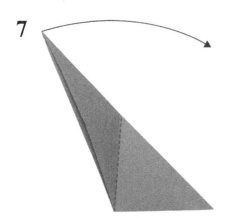

7

Make a fold.

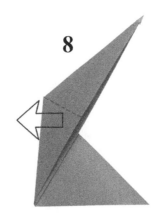

8

Unfold the corner.

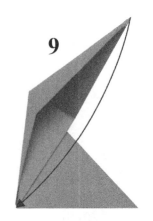

9

Fold the angle down.

10

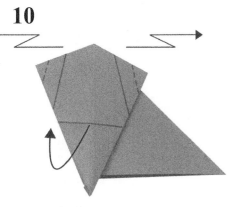

Fold the corners.

11

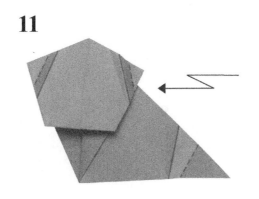

Fold the tail.

12

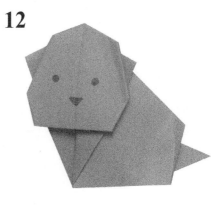

Draw a face.

#36 Dove
Basic shape - Arrow

1

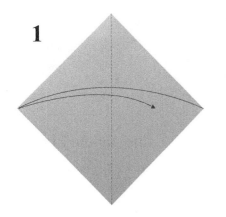

2

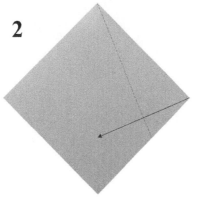

Fold the sides of the
square to the fold line.

3

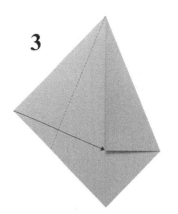

4

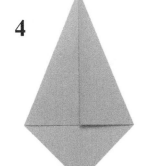

5

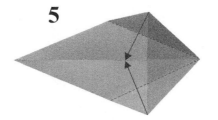

Fold the lower sides to
the center.

6

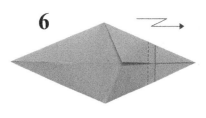

Fold the folding angle.

7

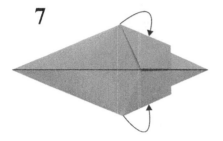

Fold up the mountain (edges down and the middle up).

8

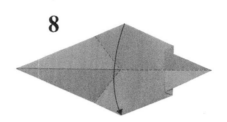

Fold in half with the fold up.

9

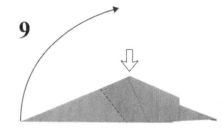

Fold the corner up and open.

10

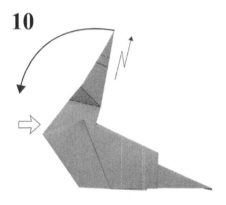

Open, fold the sharp corner of the folding and unfold.

11

Fold the folds.

12

Complete the figure.

#37 Moth

Basic shape - Double triangle

1

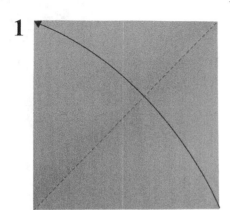

Fold the square into a triangle.

2

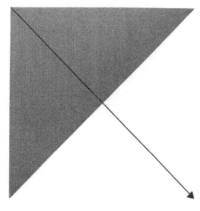

Unfold.

3

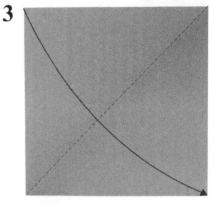

Fold the square into a triangle at another angle.

4

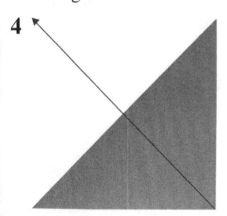

Unfold.

5

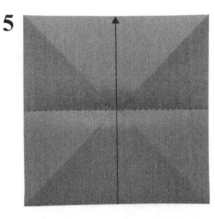

Fold the square in half.

6

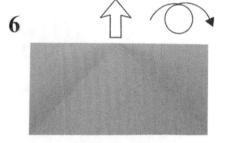

Open and turn over.

7

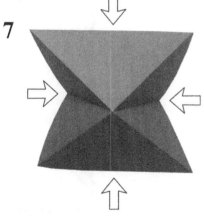

Open the shape along the fold lines.

8

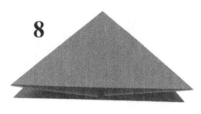

9

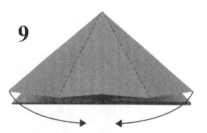

Fold the upper corners.

10

Done.

#38 Fish

Basic shape - Double triangle

1

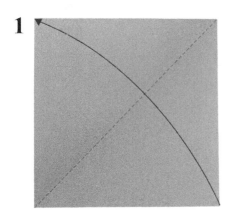

Fold the square into a triangle.

2

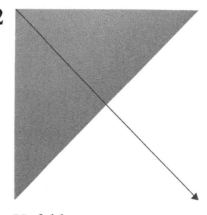

Unfold.

3

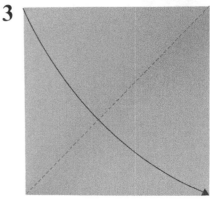

Fold the square into a triangle at another angle.

4

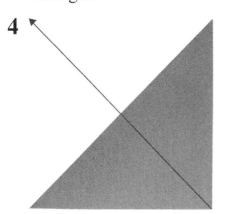

Unfold.

5

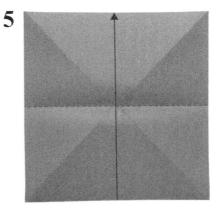

Fold the square in half.

6

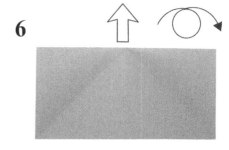

Open and turn over.

7

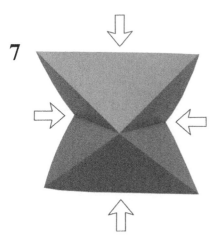

Open the shape along the fold lines.

8

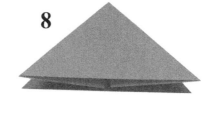

9

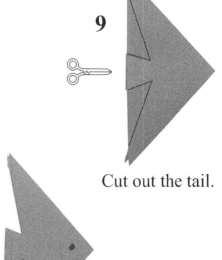

Cut out the tail.

10

Fold the incisions inwards.

11

Color the fish.

#39 Butterfly
Basic shape - Double triangle

1

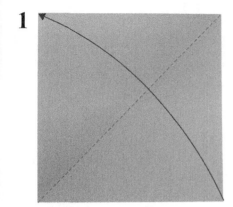

Fold the square into a triangle.

2

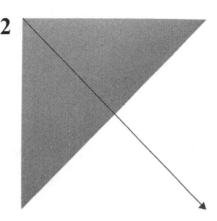

Unfold.

3

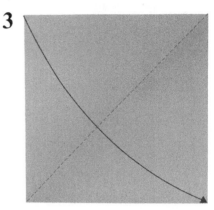

Fold the square into a triangle at another angle.

4

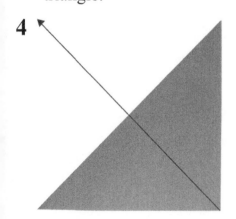

Unfold.

5

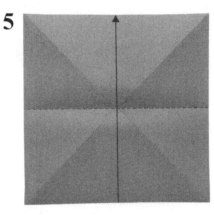

Fold the square in half.

6

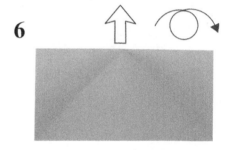

Open and turn over.

7

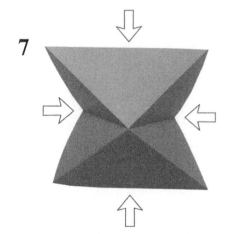

Open the shape along the fold lines.

8

9

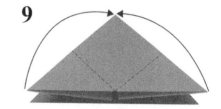

Fold the corners up to the top.

10

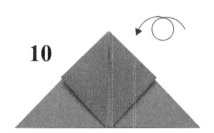

Turn over

11

Fold the corner above the edge.

12

Fold the corner.

13

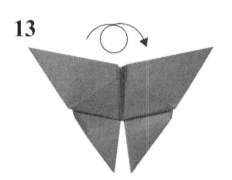

Turn the shape over.

14

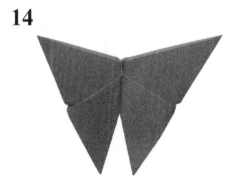

The butterfly is ready.

#40 Lily
Basic shape - Double triangle

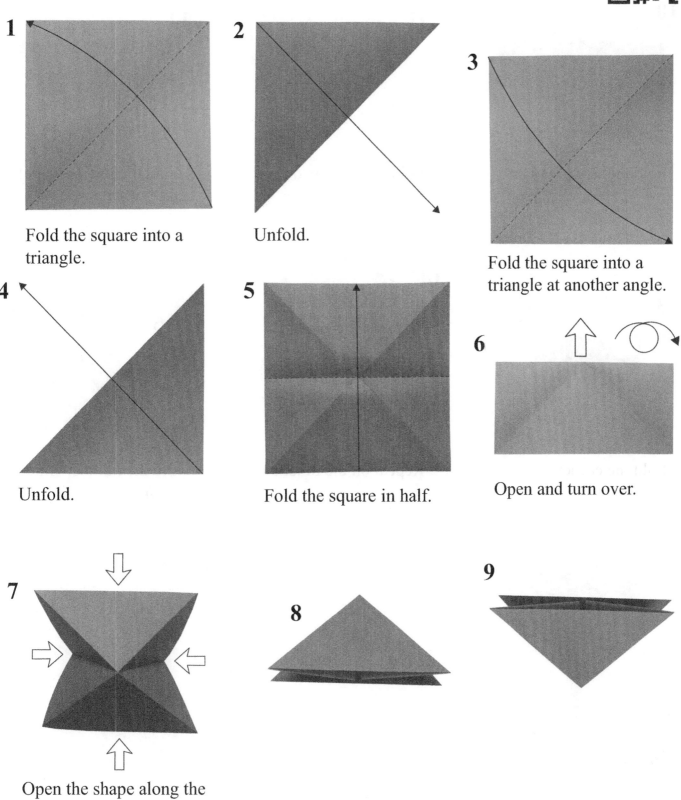

1 Fold the square into a triangle.

2 Unfold.

3 Fold the square into a triangle at another angle.

4 Unfold.

5 Fold the square in half.

6 Open and turn over.

7 Open the shape along the fold lines.

8

9

10

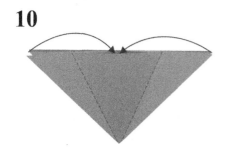

Fold the upper corners.

11

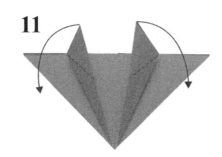

Fold the corners down.

12

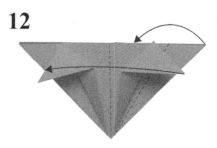

Fold the top part and fold the corner.

13

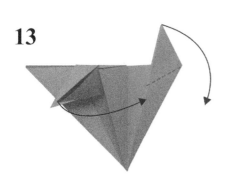

Fold the corner.

14

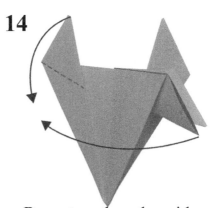

Repeat on the other side.

15

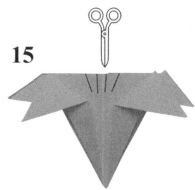

Cut the middle. Glue the stem.

16

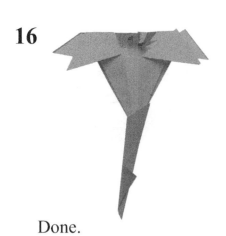

Done.

#41 Basket

Basic shape - Double triangle

1
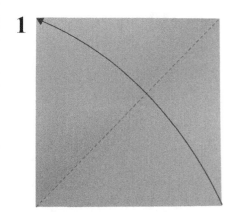
Fold the square into a triangle.

2
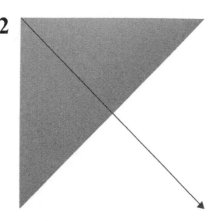
Unfold.

3
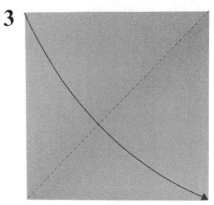
Fold the square into a triangle at another angle.

4
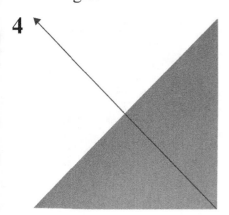
Unfold.

5
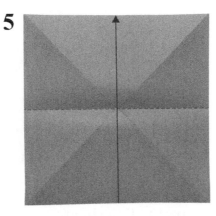
Fold the square in half.

6
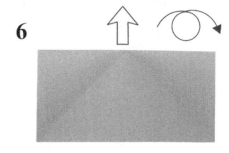
Open and turn over.

7
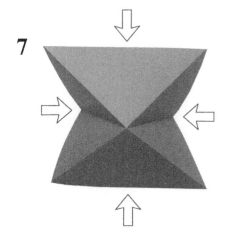
Open the shape along the fold lines.

8

9
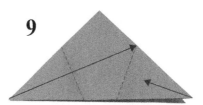
Fold the left corner to the right side. Fold right to left.

10

Tuck one into the other.

11

Turn it over.

12

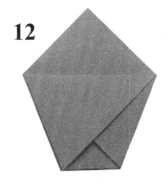

Fold up the corners as well.

13

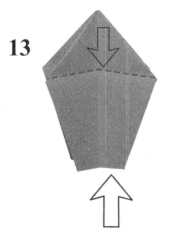

Fold the top corner down
and open.

14

Straighten the bottom
part with a square.

15

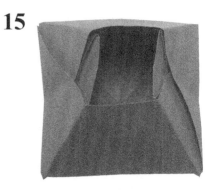

The basket is ready, glue
the handle.

#42 Tulip
Basic shape - Double triangle

1

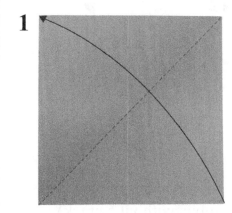

Fold the square into a triangle.

2

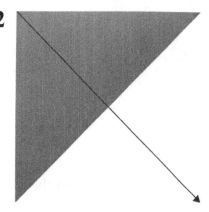

Unfold.

3

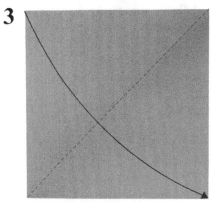

Fold the square into a triangle at another angle.

4

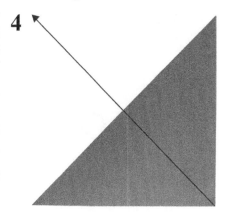

Unfold.

5

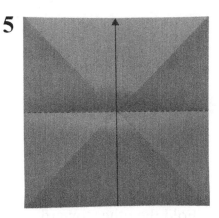

Fold the square in half.

6

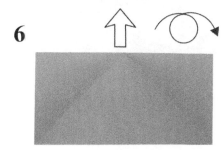

Open and turn over.

7

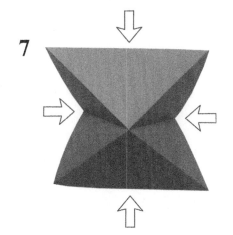

Open the shape along the fold lines.

8

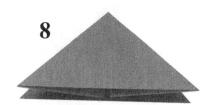

9

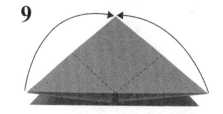

Fold the corners up to the top.

10

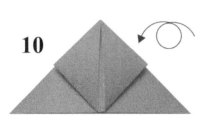

Turn over.

11

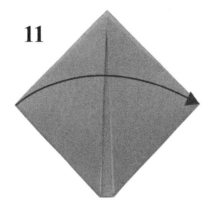

Fold the corners up to the top. Turn one part over.

12

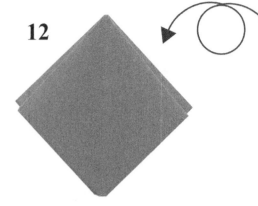

Turn over, and turn over the part (rhombus without a crack).

13

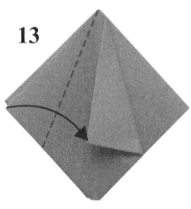

Fold the edge with a slit to the middle with an arrow.

14

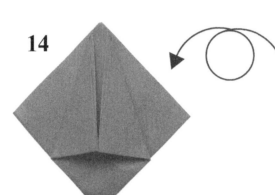

Fold the other towards and tuck in. Turn it over.

15

Also make an arrow and inflate

16

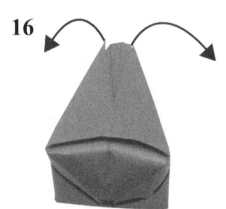

Straighten the corners from above like petals.

17

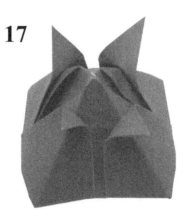

The tulip is ready. Make a stalk.

#43 Cube
Basic shape - Double triangle

1

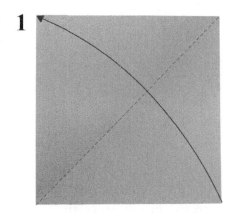

Fold the square into a triangle.

2

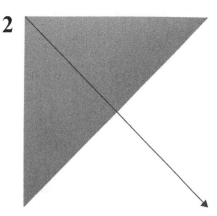

Unfold.

3

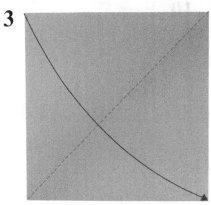

Fold the square into a triangle at another angle.

4

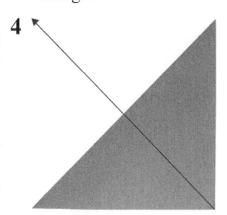

Unfold.

5

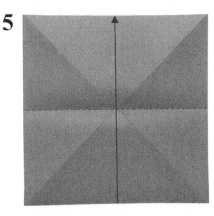

Fold the square in half.

6

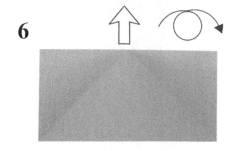

Open and turn over.

7

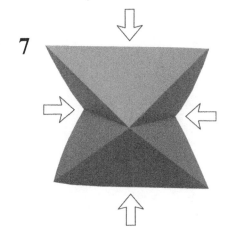

Open the shape along the fold lines.

8

9

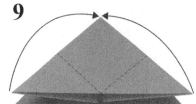

Fold the corners up to the top.

63

10

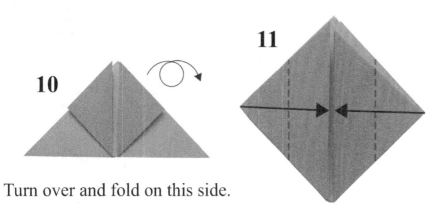

Turn over and fold on this side.

11

Fold the corners to the center.

12

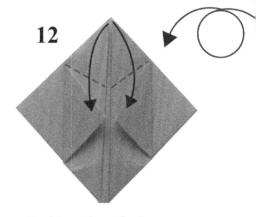

Fold and tuck the corners into the crack on both sides. Turn it over.

13

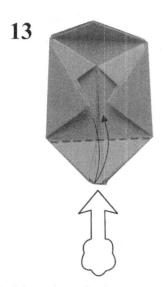

14

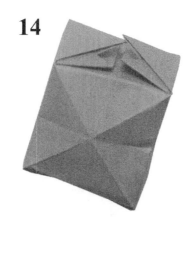

Fold and tuck the corners and fold the corners from the top and bottom.
Inflate and fold the ribs beautifully.

#44 Cow

Basic shape - Double triangle

1

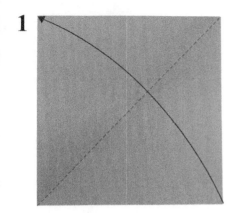

Fold the square into a triangle.

2

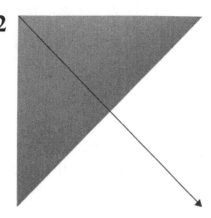

Unfold.

3

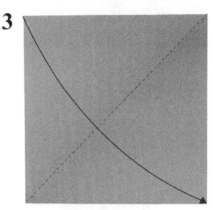

Fold the square into a triangle at another angle.

4

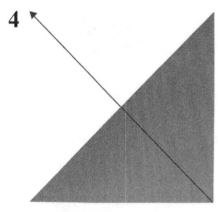

Unfold.

5

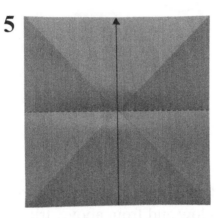

Fold the square in half.

6

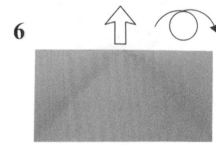

Open and turn over.

7

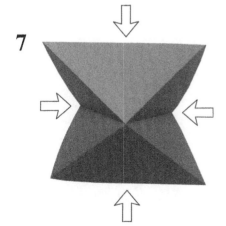

Open the shape along the fold lines.

8

9

Fold the corners up to the top.

10

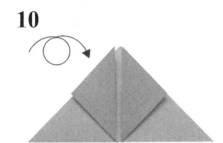

Turn over.

11

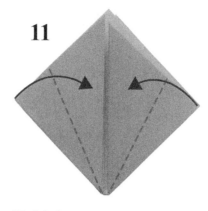

Fold the corners up to the top and fold the sides with an arrow.

12

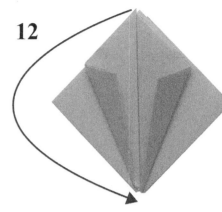

Turn 180 degrees over.

13

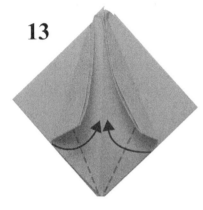

Fold the arrow towards.

14

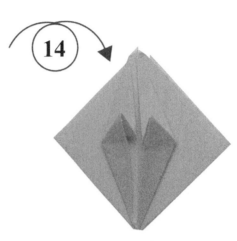

Bending at the same time from below and from above, triangles will be obtained in the middle. Turn it over and repeat too.

15

Hold the figure by these triangles on one side only and inflate the shape.

16

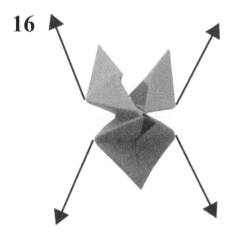

Straighten the ears and horns, pulling the corners.

17

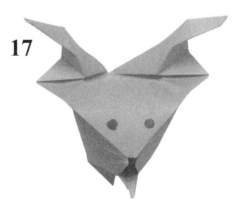

Draw the eyes.

66

#45 Vase
Basic shape - Double triangle

1

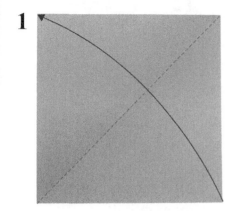

Fold the square into a triangle.

2

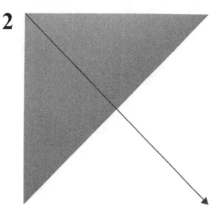

Unfold.

3

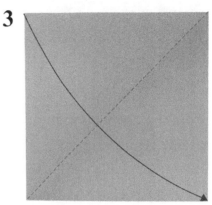

Fold the square into a triangle at another angle.

4

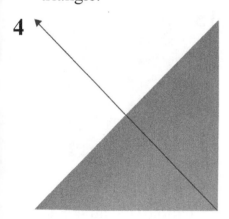

Unfold.

5

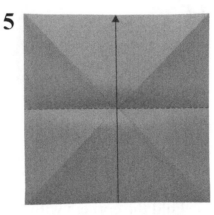

Fold the square in half.

6

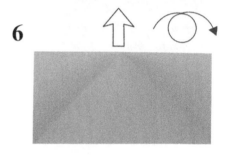

Open and turn over.

7

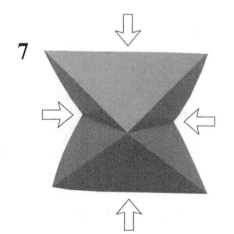

Open the shape along the fold lines.

8

9

10

Fold the corners on top of each other.

11

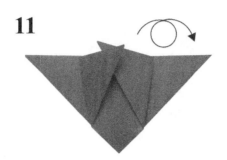

Turn over.

12

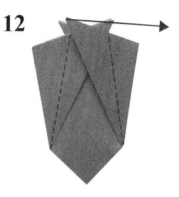

Fold the corners and fold them in half.

13

Unfold the corners and flatten. Fold them in half.

14

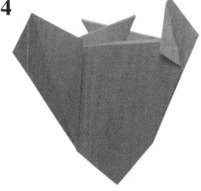

Fold the corners with the arrow inwards.

15

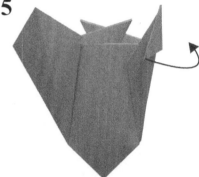

Unfold. Do all 4 sides. Fold the bottom part.

16

17

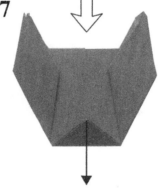

Open and straighten the base of the vase.

18

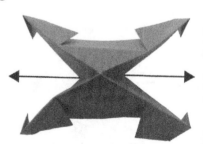

Pull from the inside to the sides.

19

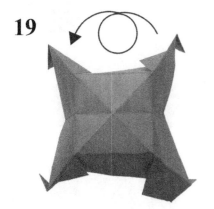

Turn over.

20

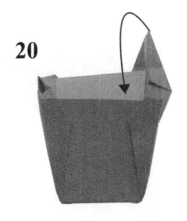

Tuck the corners inside.

21

Straighten the vase.

#46 Church

Basic shape - Double triangle

1

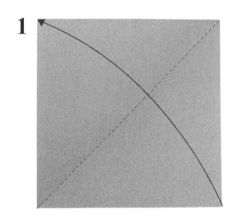

Fold the square into a triangle.

2

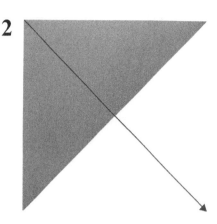

Unfold.

3

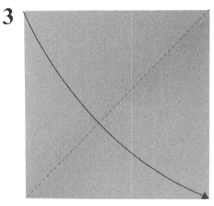

Fold the square into a triangle at another angle.

4

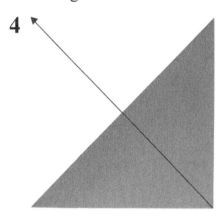

Unfold.

5

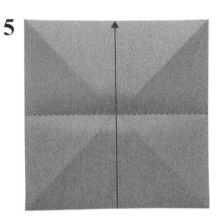

Fold the square in half.

6

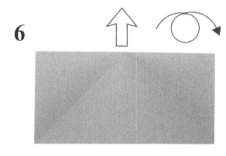

Open and turn over.

7

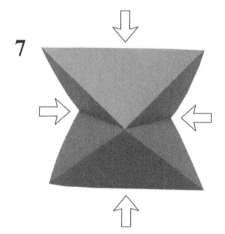

Open the shape along the fold lines.

8

9

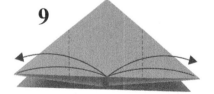

Fold the corners vertically and straighten.

10

Lift up to the middle of the figure.

11

Fold one part.

12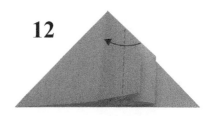

Fold in half and fold back.

13

Fold the second side.

14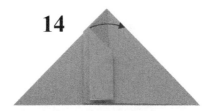

Fold in half and back.

15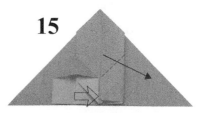

Straighten out one layer, you will get a triangle like a roof.

16

Straighten on the other side and lift the corner in the middle.

17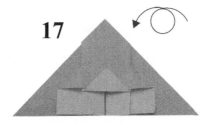

Turn over.

18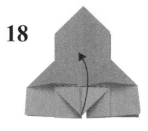

Repeat everything from this side.

19

Color it.

#47 Crane
Basic shape - Double square

1

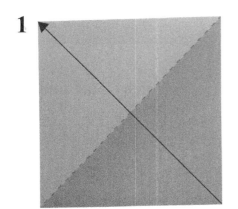

Fold the triangle.

2

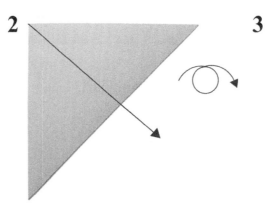

Unfold and turn over.

3

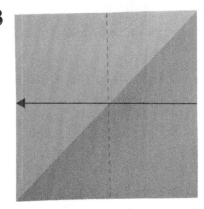

Fold the square in half lengthwise.

4

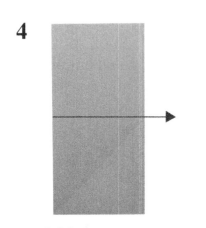

Unfold.

5

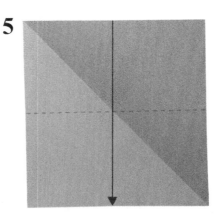

Fold the square in half across.

6

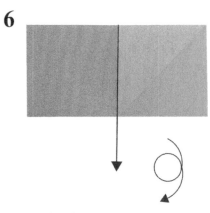

Unfold and turn over.

7

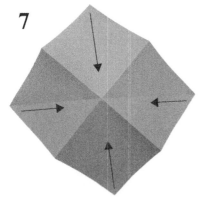

Fold along the fold lines.

8

9

Fold the sides to the center with the arrow.

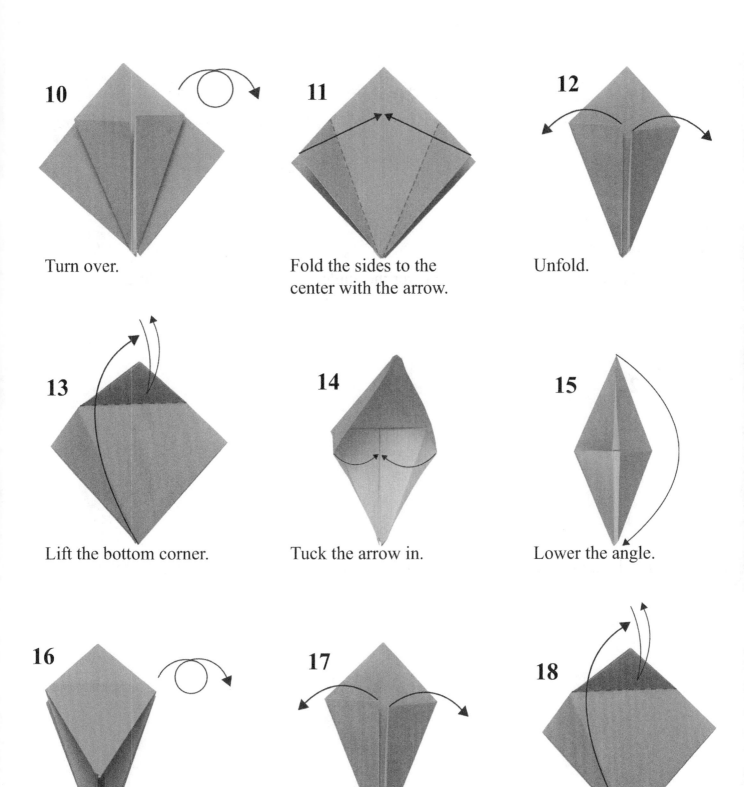

10

Turn over.

11

Fold the sides to the
center with the arrow.

12

Unfold.

13

Lift the bottom corner.

14

Tuck the arrow in.

15

Lower the angle.

16

Turn over and repeat
from 12 to 15.

17

Unfold.

18

Lift the bottom corner.

19

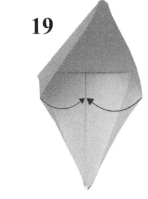

Tuck the arrow in.

20

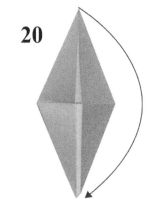

Lower the angle.

21

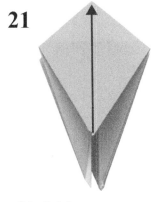

Unfold.

22

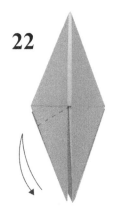

Fold and unfold.

23

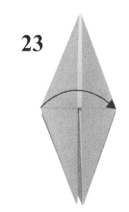

Fold the folds.

24

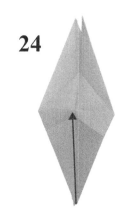

Fold the folds.

25

Fold over the folds.

26

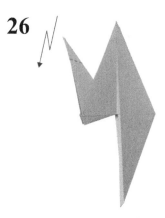

Fold the corner like a beak.

27

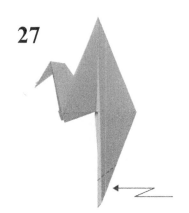

Fold the tip at the bottom like a leg.

28

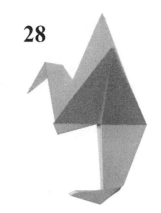

The crane is ready.

#48 Crab
Basic shape - Double square

1

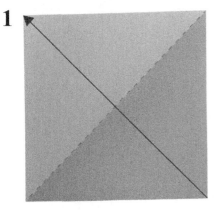

Fold the triangle.

2

Unfold and turn over.

3

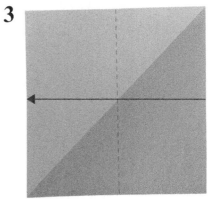

Fold the square in half lengthwise.

4

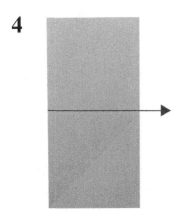

Unfold.

5

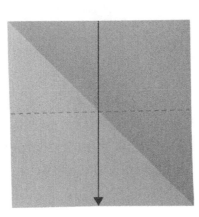

Fold the square in half across.

6

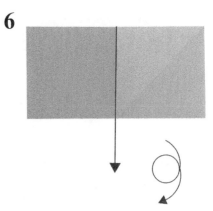

Unfold and turn over.

7

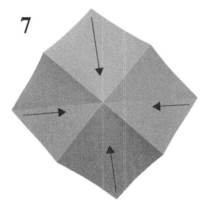

Open along the fold
lines.

8

9

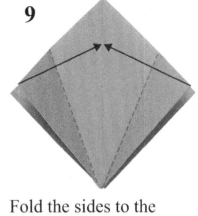

Fold the sides to the
center with the arrow.

10

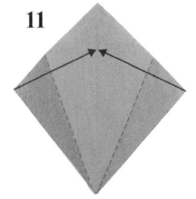

Turn over.

11

Fold the sides to the
center with the arrow.

12

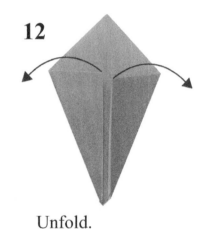

Unfold.

13

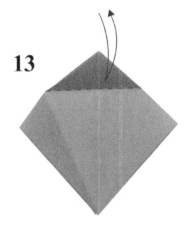

Fold and unfold the
upper corner.

14

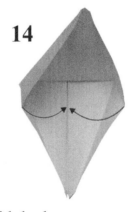

Fold the bottom corner
and tuck the arrow in.

15

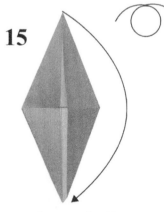

Lower the angle. Turn
over and repeat from 12
to 15.

16

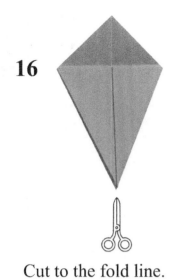

Cut to the fold line.

17

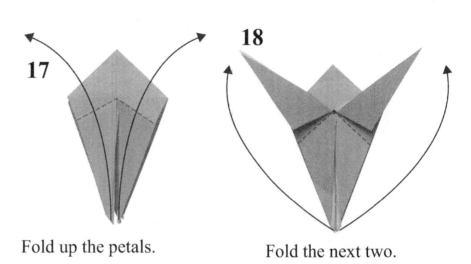

Fold up the petals.

18

Fold the next two.

19

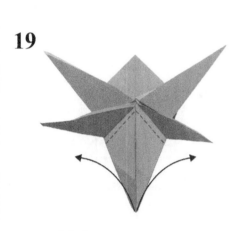

Fold the next two.

20

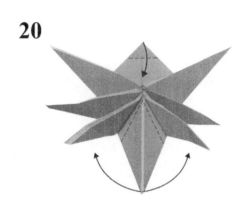

Fold the next two and fold the corner from the top.

21

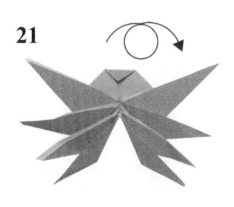

Turn over.

22

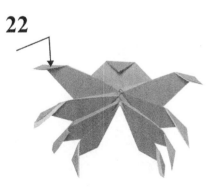

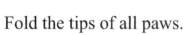

Fold the tips of all paws.

23

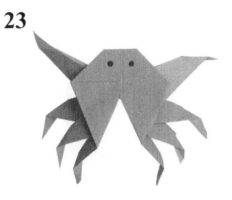

The crab is ready to draw the eyes.

#49 Maple leaf
Basic shape - Double square

1

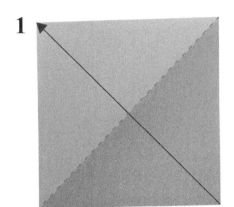

Fold the triangle.

2

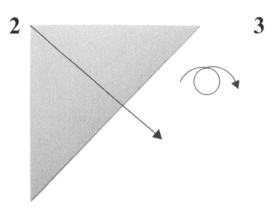

Unfold and turn over.

3

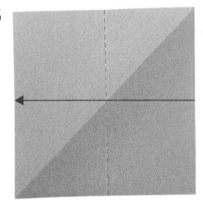

Fold the square in half lengthwise.

4

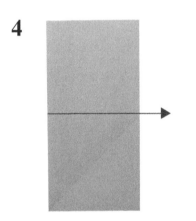

Unfold.

5

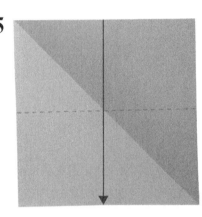

Fold the square in half across.

6

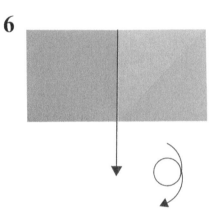

Unfold and turn over.

7

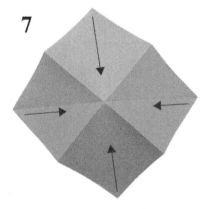

Open along the fold lines.

8

9

Fold the sides to the center with the arrow.

10

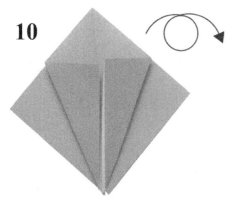

Turn over.

11

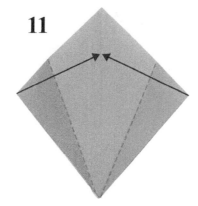

Fold the sides to the center with the arrow.

12

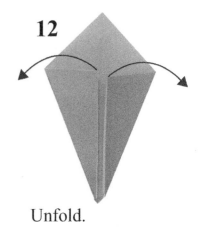

Unfold.

13

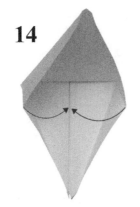

Fold and unfold the upper corner.

14

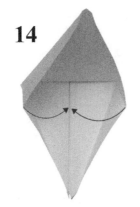

Fold the bottom corner and tuck the arrow in.

15

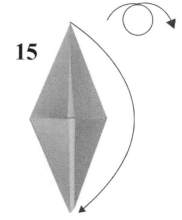

Lower the angle. Turn over and repeat from 12 to 15.

16

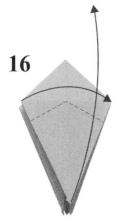

Fold up the petal and flip through.

17

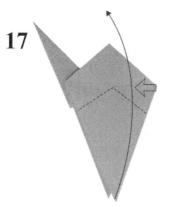

Fold the front up and close to the left.

18

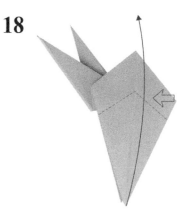

Fold the front up and close to the left.

79

19

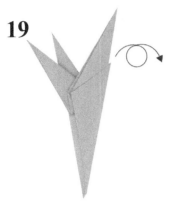

Turn over.

20

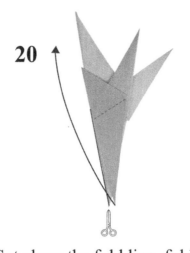

Cut along the fold line, fold up.

21

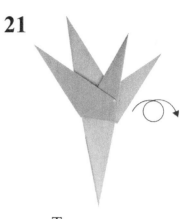

Turn over.

22

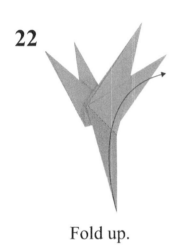

Fold up.

23

The sheet is ready.

24

Glue the stalk.

#50 Frog

Basic shape - Double square

1

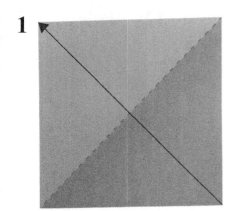

Fold the triangle.

2

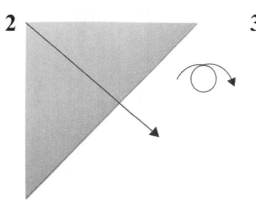

Unfold and turn over.

3

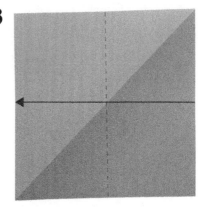

Fold the square in half lengthwise.

4

Unfold.

5

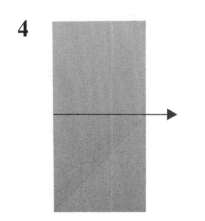

Fold the square in half across.

6

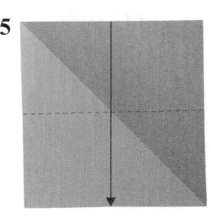

Unfold and turn over.

7

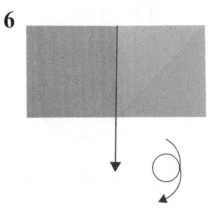

Open along the fold lines.

8

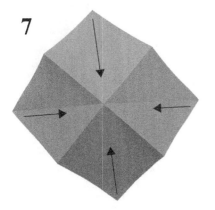

9

Fold the sides to the center with the arrow from the fold side.

81

10

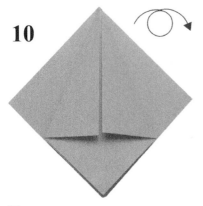

Turn over.

11

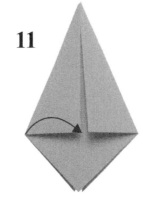

Unfold one part.

12

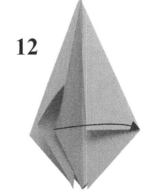

Fold the triangle.

13

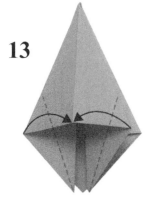

Fold the sides to the center.

14

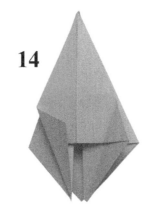

Unfold.

15

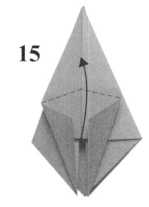

Lift the middle up.

16

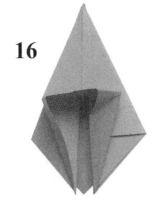

Straighten the triangle.

17

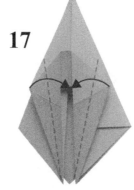

Fold the sides to the center.

18

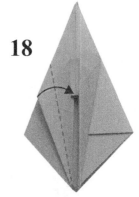

Both sides.

19

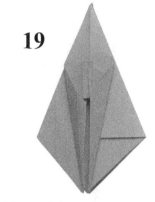

Close this part.

20

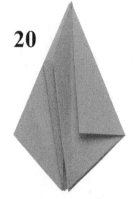

Unfold the next part and repeat from 12 to 19.

21

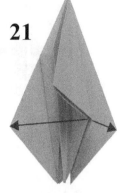

Do these manipulations with all sides.

22

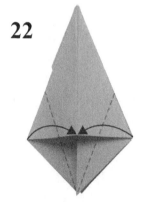

Fold the sides to the center.

23

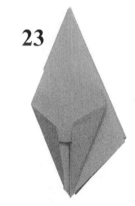

Unfold.

24

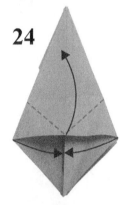

Fold the middle up. Straighten the triangle.

25

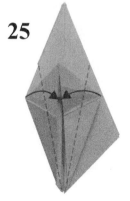

Fold the sides to the center.

26

Both sides.

27

Fold and open the next triangle.

28

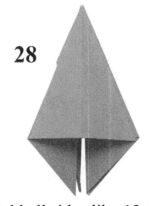

Fold all sides like 13 to 19 or 20 to 27.

29

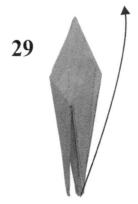

Unfold and fold.

30

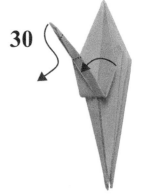

Fold up the foot.

31

Unfold.

32

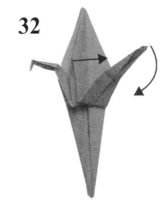

Fold the tip 2 times.

33

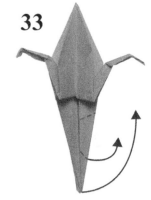

Fold the foot on the other side.

34

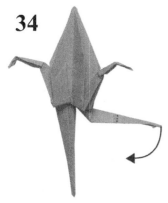

Fold the lower legs.

35

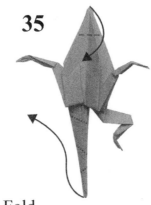

Fold.

36

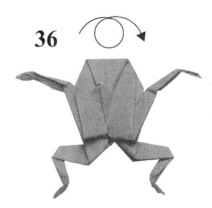

Turn over.

37

Done.

ALL VIDEOS (Playlist)

All videos are also in the same playlist on YouTube:

or Link:

cutt.ly/8KKsMC1

Messages about typos, errors, inaccuracies and suggestions for improving the quality are gratefully received at: kostyayaroshenkocat@gmail.com

Thank you for your recent purchase. *We hope you will love it!* If you can, would you consider posting an online review? This will help us continue to provide great products and help potential buyers make confident decisions.

Thank you in advance for your review and for being a preferred customer.

The most popular musical instrument in the world is the piano. You can also try an easy and simple training from my colleague Avgusta Udartseva.

Check out her book:

Made in the USA
Las Vegas, NV
03 November 2024

11052513R00050